Recap

Poems

by

R. Vincent Razor

VERNOX Publishing, Queens NY 11415

Library of Congress Cataloging-in-Publication Data
1991, 1992, 1993, 1994, 1995, 1996, 1997, 1998, 1999,
Recap

ISBN-13: 978-0-9786682-1-1
ISBN-10: 0-9786682-1-9

VERNOX
PO Box 150308
Kew Gardens
New York 11415-0308

contents

humanity's steps

silhouette!
the eye of the storm is cast
upon the emaciate sorrow
a haunting specter soliloquize the dark:
"timber!
rage the fallen tree
uprooted;
all humanity humbles
before the soul of its imprint-
there is thunder!
nearly distinct
then gone
the pallid tremble whimpers
of orchids and children mad without play
of whores and junkies crushed without pity
the unnimble cripple rises from his unfettered grave
to seize the dying wind!
to capture again the naked spirit
of life and death and immortality
bridge the storm between lilies and thunder
perdition reigns supreme!
begging the wind to shadow remains
but not for its own fecund
a command for a nation to rise
from its darkest depths
a mystery torn from its bloodiest womb
now this blood on lilies appeals
to the greater passive sanguine mist
seeps time's empty gullet
poverty unsurge!
prophets surmise!
let the weight of a soul, its worth
pound back nature's mightiest force
crash the rocks of eternity's matter
where love and paradox mock survive
and tranquility assumes its natural play!"

dark beauty

matter!
the awesome silence of stone
speaks -
a word,death
of life
-something,
-now!

comes civilization -
whining on its "ditty" comfort-rancor
all drunk with stupid vocal
slurring onto history's incurable tract
of seltzer and soul bubbly dark
seasons whimper hordes
of wild wisdom failed restraint,unfinished
tears resting,heart murmur
quietly pounding last vicious beat
from scribe peers -bum;
all seasons past
now comes the revelation-appeal
maybe?
he holds the mystery
close to eternity's most private encounter
inordinate dark bares beauty -full content
in smouchy-lip-smacking pursuit
all hot and slutty buss
on perpetuity's wet back and front
widely parting these moistful tender folds
into the prosti'-thrashing debacle
of virtue less than timorous
but great aspirations contempt
atop mountains made level
absolution's misused power,
so egregious buffoonery
yet to rest,
dying to rest;
to the trees in the forest
belongs -

look deep
into particle incumbent
fueled energy abate!
destiny contracts and expands
partisan view complete,
nonsense persists -
indelible tractable anomalies

puzzle-out extraordinary circumstance;
the pity and isolation
of firm resolve and tapestries
laid bare threads essential,
torn-
patterns nature's necessity preserve -
deep and accountable
smoke riddling through cracks
his fingers scorched -
knotted,skilled,tendered,
by age's unskillful drag
through time's unkindest street
now succumbs
gladly -reluctantly
soul bared -barred -
dark sky's deepest vat
of wine undrunk
never reveled,
unpartied,yet
to come a memory serving
autocratic invisibility
made visible again,
with circumstance
direct,
final,
obsolescent -

fashion genius -
recalcitrant promises
void,counter point!
again scorned beauty
marks its direst post,
secluding memory from altruism's
most profound sense of dispose;
commonality professes of season's muster;
the plain and simple speak
cornered,spoken,
alternatives,unpossessed
now solicits:
come heart -
murmuring and pitying toy
bleed the aching sense of this mystery
into this unknown dark
variety,discovery,yield -
evolution harvests
immense universe -unpack!?
cornucopi' all the angel-devil-trysts
held secret captive beyond comprehension
so human,so fragile

so laughably vain -
comes this callous celebration
centuried folklore's vogue-trade
common for uncommon
in pursuit -

violins

violins
weeping,
angeled,
grieved
into utter violent repose -
still weeps,
landing,
but never succumbs
still flesh
still grieving,
flesh -

bloody uncurl
high aspirations posed,brittle-up
into soul shaped,denied
music!
contemplation's whipped reserve!
naked -
beaten over a nation
mourns this gypsy corpse
undressed for rot
and unforgiving esthetic -
pleas merciful beginnings -
triumph marched out,
oozing over all
beauty's clay melting
grey-wrinkling excess
at peeling this scarred shell
age's pitiful pouting reaper
grim of rage and cowardice -lost!
snotty-distilled,horror-mocking,creeping death,untriumphs
slow-dancing into loathesome's country undig' resolve
flames burning,particular youth
uncompromising,still burning
repugnant but unkneebending
dissolves -
but continues -

fugue -
new time unwarps
music -
reality harsh
deafening,everything soundful death
climbing out of its tuneless womb
quickly stunned to knees
by sweetly harrowing notes

meticulous soul's extract
departed weanling precipice
innately guarding
human aspiration evolved
to the higher element reaper so grim
its ravenous thrashing of flesh
to pieces scattered dust
falls to the prevails -
insistent decadent discard
victory's bitter brief
recalls,lost precipice,lost
culmination's uncommon ride
hosts -
wizened immensurable unsolace
askance perpetuity's lock on dark
saddled wind,soaring notes
against flesh to soul to universe
equation absolute
ultimate merge -
absolute
propose -

capturing grief
sullen,
noble winds -
content,
rising perseverant
new league dubious of spirit
now soul's depth's unlet
flooding
earth's other waves character linked
rising,
above the line
evolution's aspirations,commonality,
distant   -but rising,
notes all pleasing elicitations
grander expectations
soaring pinnacled anticipation
stated,
absolute -

the juggler

on trial!
sovereignty expounds!
the juggler juggles;
a curious trick of balance -
a state's fecund -absolute!
an independent,out-of-season delish';
the ripest picking of succulent fruits and troublesome quarry
between the darker cast of condemnation,
confrontation breeding -
and air of embattled difference,rife
with blood and acceptance mixed and turned
rushing through arteries cut-growth for blossom,
pertains -

in this court of courts
high humanity burgeons
with full fruited convict'
above sky and soul intended,
arc of magic surmise
these preternatural spirits curse
of sub-substance and regal blind shatter
deep into the source,transcendent manifest
a cold,dark,awesome pity
of slobbering angels
all dogfight bloody and hungered
of satan-demons snow-purity driven
all frothy dancing wedded bliss
on light-back illusion create
composites:
the iron willed doctrine
of junk-book text
ram bashing against fired air impervious
to history's raging bull locking horns
over the heresy of humanity sleeping,
slumbering on its own primordial watch
in the green of nature's anarchy veld
turning red of war and mistrial
making odious,grotesque and uninhabitable
the face of soul and discreet pardon
still placid accept
the juggler,this master of illusion
forms his greatest arc -

and this trial,its peers,gather the show
acquitted on all counts
he continues to astound

treaty

broken!
morning glory!
crimson glory!
out of stone -
out of soul -
out of naked exist
bares its ultimate denial -
war!

mourning glory
risen above everything
blue in all but fusing blooming
bleeds the stem uncut
stands a petrified chief in field
red ordered,centuried,soul unshaved
bowed white glory,unbroken
perpetuity high,marks the rings
once flesh,
now stands alone -

the smallest acorn planted -bursts!
the dawn and chameleon headdress wail full fury
shattering rainbows casted skies unparted
lightning golden
god of thunder bows and kneels in humbled awe
of misery much out lasted
of sorrow's grain of wheat too weeviled
out of ear and bands
armed this heathen warrior
digging for lost tribes justice
unquenched thirst for unity
unlost upon the healing river's dig 'nity
running through soul and unborn trees to come
fetal renown,treaty yet broken
ever so deep
the roots into a nation's soul breed its rising
and history's fall never failing -
there is triumph!

body of human,
soul of eternity
spirit of the beating heart -
pack-rabid hounds turning moon,untied
begin to gait!

the ferocious flaming winds fles

upon all chiefs,warriors,women and children
and phantoms gather ;!;round the fired eve
of telling white smoke engulfs,up transcends
the hoary blood-living reverberation
on the brown-dead of lands and destinies manifest
a trial,smoke rising
into perpetuity's infinite charm -unmasked!
into war! incisors cut!
deep through tendon and bone
these wild dogs spit out gristled failure's
achieve,mock-survive!
leaving history's torn limb and lame,
limping toward endless retelling
lies upon the corpse,without the blooming
without the carnage prized,ascendent
relinquishing the hawk's pervious dive
into hell's plummetless depths
breeds in its belly
an apostheosis wings from the darkest depths
of the blackest,hairiest beast
to the supreme white cloud spirits
high in the most resplendent incarnate
without the rabbit's ears twitching
winds this soul
back into exist!

domicile

midnight!
the circle forms -
silence rebounds;
depth's fierced-inception,dreams embrace
raise an eaglet to the moon
peers!
plummet -
the knife!
soul and flesh divide!
dying embers -
extract!
from destiny's dark oak
here assembled under one munificent sphering gorge
these wishing spirits undo a god
pyred;
ashen;
risen-

civilization -ungrieve!
a nation's souls up-fading,up-dark
up-black! to docile mourning peril
from history's passive blood-spitting wretch
something terribly naked-
queasing,dissolution spirit
forming unprivate,unpitying night
hold! risen moon!
first clean,
the bird child!
unfeathered,
unfleshed;
unscarred by touch!
again manifest
unruffled feathers
fly raw without eternal view
now
doctrine initiate!

up-state!
up whimpering solemn amenities
of tyranny and clinging memory
both dribbling bowels released and unforgiven
simultaneously obstructing
truth's undeniable flush
remains unconvinced
in the fierced demon-eagle eyes extant
engulfing crater and mountain and dust

in blood and flesh -and bone
marrowed deep in the sanguinary necessity of war
exists this new soul
discovered,robus,achieved -

cradled in this haggard bosom
hordes of death premiere
riding high on the feathered appaloosa
trotting confidently dark
near perilous dancing ocean's rocks
a shore beginnings back
receding as far as far as life extant
unfailing peace resolve
a gathering;
exogenous patterns in shadows
outside this law,this storm,
memories
carcinogens reprise!
chant!
chant!

morning reprise!
vintage doctrine unveil!
pierced soul succumb
dive eagle,dive!
plummet the bowels earth intent
claw-catch the rodent nocturne feed
beak-out the morsel strips
humanity's well stuffed refrain
feasted the all purposed soul
outside the laws
orbited on the out-outs
still centured within the center
larceny betrays the heart
the stolen kisses surrender
still uncaught -
still puckered
still pretended
ostent!

gash!
the fettered soul bleeds
still human
still unwinged,
magnificent!
mourning -

monarch

'stilled
of smoke and gold
descent -

soul tendered
unwished constrict -
'tombed in winter's cowardice ice
magnificent unaltered wings
of tiger-bursting suns
deep seas construct
so tinged of blood
captured raw
royal fettered rainbows
now cast punctured lungs,cold
blue moon,
tyrant

deceived
brutal genius,
whores and kings -chipping
winter-century code embrace
sloppy to the knees contritions
wretching atrophy -splitting purity rock
ungrasped in thinking total
deified beyond natural select
codified in enemy delusions
splendid shackled grandure
too fat and unrepentant
brittle royal saber bones
cut for rattling anarchy;
vengeance shield,
covered in primal evil
smothered preternatural concupiscence
breaking royal bloody stone -
hacking into social venue hysteric
in this winged stabbing block
sacrificed impermanence -
in this dark,velvet-luring,obsequious shimmer
full moon gorged in flames
a scorched soul dripping
royal tempests unconstruct,
royal winged crown
dissolves -

island

rank!
air-fossiled!
blood-wind ascent -
driven!

thunder risen!
thunder fallen!
angel teardrops,flaming doves,
wing-lightning breeding,
shower-seeding,wind-fired yellowed gods,
soaring full-souled
spiral down
quick-rain
sharp shift
shrowding lush anarchy
green island center,wet
violent
violet
ageless fecund purple violet
dark/light
sanguinary pause
now mooned -

pace
brinking velvet jungle
trembles into island-focal trancing
history's sweet linking revenge
repeats -

bloomed-
a wind-shaped infected flower
deep breathing sigh,empathetic dreams
heaving eternity's briefest fling -
thrashing civilization out
from one form,
into another -
blowing seeds,randomly
lived,fought,died
sparked again
aspired,
risen -

off the line -
perpetuity's lost decency
trashed decadent resolve
stripped flesh

from too babied innocence
flayed raw,then smoked
into a foul kicking exchange
between naked goddy aspiration
and civilization's actual caterpillar crawl
both green-runny scabby-kneed invasion
coward under a pathetic cleft-lipped,stammer-lisping smile
while decay-inching into yet one more generation
of ordinary paradox
and unordinary frenetic leaping
with bizarre untrackable moves
this majestic soul-shifting spector
so visioned
so unclear,
so contemptuously pursued
manifests-
all sins blown over-
a frail,deeply rooted violet,
not so fragile;
unstormed by external veraties-
exists -

a bee
buzzing,this flower blossomed
an irritant dissolved
by future's inevitable suck
into the past
dark corner universe
here exists this soul,
particle chip all built
and decimated before the new dawn
the buzz resonates
the bee does not
the flower continues
to bloom again,
pollinated wind and more islands
again -

breach

breach!
in the silent womb of treason
in the dark wings of a soul's manifest
in the symphony trades of nature's desperate urgings
bornes a seed;
a whore's extrapolate
stringed and tympanied -
pulsing,
a passion's unconscionable rise,
a nucleus;
gathering its traitorous flesh
culling its saddling periodicity
breeding,slowly -completely,
attach!
flash!
shock!
birth!
-exigent

mournful calibration-
life!
mournful separation-
death!
pride futures determined-
fetal inclinations denied!
syncopation pities delectable hour
grad' absolute momentum
nature's briefest tenure
devise and revised its own schematic counter
point from angel seed -
to devil polemic fruition
a gathering of soul from core
from those desperate urging symphonies
wings chorus one!   -demanding the build -
of a moment!
embodied in a singular,elemental note
for the times
for all time,
again

linked!
to peer   the library gene
by reason infinite significant trust
a burgeon of flowering matter
in dusty pollen thought

sprinkles on fringe comparable notes
leaped once that tragically truncated recall
that prim novice of experience
lacking more will,courage
and undisciplined bravado
comes a breach of instance
in that intimate specificity
broken down to spec
of thought,
then
bang!
acceleration!
nature's silent duty
caughing up a key to that womb of knowledge
into a pit of swirling generalities
slowly,forming,still connected
quietly coordinating
into that pool of unfathomed calibrations
one soul to expectedly succeed the next
as perceived
by other subtleties
still forming,
nova
again,
-exigent

breaking grounds

diseased!
cured!
cored!
fated!
of soul and blood
magnificent mountain cat
whisper-clawed-out corticine blue;
dripping elemental spirit dead
open-totem-wooden artery
covering the morals slash,royal
wearing grief,judgement dark;
eternity on blind shocking bright
these piercing eyes shive
hawking extract-
screeching the shaking unwarring lamb-slaughter honor
on this ignominious departure
from tree,to man,to a god on boundary
stands these linear multi-gods
unmasked - one!
sight far perpetuity back
of soul face to soul
to face
to necessity,gods created
river likeness reflect
carved purpose,
existence,too -

god of winter,melting
god of spring,beginning
god summer,still warring
god of fall,now succumb
to life -
under these boulder-wintered,blood-fertiled plains
the essence of civilization
seeps up from death-laden earth's everything grasp
division between iron back
and immortality's sepulcher contingent
siege of soul on brink-life-death
quietly slipping into forever's
undisguised natural selection
deep host imminent harmony elements
this secretive selection,so nature
so dark season cruel delusion
fiercely inaugurates
perpetuity's lame,torn,
unmercied,half eaten,cast aside

the weakies burgeon these grounds
fecund immortal gods,mortal cuts
fashioned on necessity's bear grizzly
battled,skinned,prized;
victory's benevolent slow thaw
forgives the imbroglio's bitter trech'
allowing spoil's savage sweet savor
to trickle blood drip
off all trails
leading to all paths,
forgotten -
natively begged

flesh!
spirit!
a god is born -
solicitous ceremony,open wounded ferret
chiefly gnawing dried skin and berry
now springs to harmony rash-fisted decadence
silhouette -breakout!
spirits design
ancient protocol liquids elements
disguised -unguised
breakout!
harbinger's season rabbit runs unperiled
through forests and open fields
no boundaries all innate
the mind's ventured eye
seeks resolution preservation
incumbent death
seated on the slash of unincumbent offsprings
confrontation's warriors
unsated in their primordial comings a seeing
in extraordinary particle discharge
in the chipping,breaking precipice
on the grandiose seminal simplicity
mastered unguarded and predesting
surrender to invented codes of movements
governed by invented gods to spike these moves
carried century,largely after century
in line,if not multiple conclusion
spirits course and become
generations -

sleeping with the gods

the tempests lay prostrate,still
a naked whore's bartered chant
whiskey breathes a solemn key
they rise -

struck!
their conscience attuned!
to ease a militant melody draft
music chum the seas of desperate wars
the whole of ideology crushed
under antiquity's nasty chance
unbetrayed history does not repeat!
union the gods of solidarity's reprise!
bloody attrition born of lazy solace
of incomplete dreams not transcended
the great bonds of humanity's diligence
broken,squelched unceremoniously
a lark sings with sounds unherald
in breaking morning's undistinguished perish
the dour widow beckons
mourning -
still dawn
morning -

the silence whispers,
crouched in a corner
the whimpering coddled priests
of nostalgia and regime
dutifully bow for decapitation -
horribly failed in their protracted contrition
more than a few centuries of self righteous wing-stripping
bloodless raping the virgin birds unchirped
humanity's abortion abounds
preternatural gifts of life
inbred rood,in well mannered rancid,wormy detention
of a prisoner's cell constricts
all movements society's lingering rose
petaled indifference,saturates all postumous strivings
the gift of decadence masters illusion
profound,misconceived -

tender profanity sips
a drink of wine,a drink of blood
letting their brains soaked gods of temerity
and dire circumstance,pare obscurity
ensconced in life's dreary repeat

down the shell wrapped classicist league
cracked on impact
the tedious practiced indifference
of piety shocked late century vandals
vigilantly midnight looting pharmacy soul-banks
leaning on the still human factors
maintaining a moving river's bumps and grinds
and mossy derelicts perpetually plagued veracities
mixed unfavorably in this contain
designed to wash over those persistent stubbies
then overflowing the gutters and minds
decay stagnating only the unnecessaries
cleaning the most favorably inclined
into evolution's waiting mit,
changing into the moment's moment
to whatever will uncomfortably survive
in vulgarity's knowing suspicion
that something can come from nothing
if the air is rife -
with the recalling memory of genius

the anxious face of treason glimmers -
this countenance betrays illusion
misfits of all circumstance
rant and charge the circus events
blustering and billowing
lust for pity - lust for lust
every act a creature distinct
of character and purpose
all trained to partake in the festivities
dared and not dared for fear
to survive -

the fear of fear dissipates
as purpose manifests its gender details
the evolution of the moment
precipitates all likely eventualities
there is music-pertain
the greatness of the gods
in this last ring,embody
the principles,these animals
hoist their souls up the long burning ropes,
brief the moment,
bold,unchained,
they create -
and transcend

ginger time

mercy angel
dark recumbent mass
crushed weight!
outwit -out light!
beam up upon the wings
ginger,marking break
still emanating exists
sweetly angel
dark baby dark
infant cries
sweet naked black angel
up bright!
burst!
burst baby burst!

unlit gleam
proxy yellow glowing
radiant lily burning
torpid,trepid' reflect
cunning night-fox
eyes lashing fiercely
through the heart
wildly pumping
in heat
expands -

glorious passivity
nocturnal sweet exchange
daunting task unsullied
growling ultimate manifest
whimpering child cry
petal drop,drip
ferociously,savaged night
rippled coddled start
crippled
that horrible voice
trapped!
crying out from a dead star
screaming,eternal screaming
wicked cloister
cold alter night
screaming
screaming banshee
bursting windless ill winds
scorched flesh,unfleshed

dire angel
wicked ensemble
pledge to the soul of creativity
mouthy bleedy run
punched out dark winged knight
carried
the calm,the terror
the utter chaos
incomplete,complete
paradox's unlimited purpose
storm manifest
the "i" principle
essence
catalyst
being -

more fractured lines
paths untraveled
moreover time
unfractured
unlined
continuous,
changing
unbroken,aware
total time,
absolute -
the crush
the absence of all light
birthing,breathing
one splinter
one sliver
burgeoning brighter
brighter,
brighter,
even still -

butterfly

risen wing
transcendent fix
soaring single depth
poison dark infected purpose
turns;
the sad earth
lays bare
a petal unturned,aspired;
monsters breeding more,
more open wounds laying trap
the unconscionable peril blossoms
roar -

a nation holds
the disconsolate ring of death
gathers over the ample bosom and soft under belly
of countries and boundaries
seductively disarranged,
petulant wild flowers
cast their disconcerting wilt
upon the morning glory
broken tear!
weeping pacifist tear!
dreadful,salted,anguished tear!
passionate discourse -resolve!
decadent arbitration -deploy!
opposition
arranged!

wilt!
fired fields
unharbored fields
burned out enviable wombs
conflagration clearing
the painful nobility of wither
rising to meet necessity's deniable obligations -denied!
hollow resolve -
returned!
growth!
tyranny's awful neglect
tempered,honored pernicious night
black widow's incendiary spin
the volcanic spew
once cloaking all the green and yellow crop
now the disemboweling catch

bleeding open fevered arteries
delirium's weeping laws
reveal!
freedom's benevolent dusty tomb
links
heart/history
a nation moans
the creepy spider -unnested
oozing that awful,smoky,blackened pus
covered crops
no longer great green or yearly yellow
pitiful lack convict'
but dangerously turned
revelation surprise
birth again -

the unscorched cocoon
cracks -
extreme dawn
bold,unfettered dawn
unbearably terse,blistered dawn
blossoms -shell
shell-breaks
wings
brightly rainbow contage' (contagion)
infectious color pronounce
color crimson,cut throat shimmer
royal blue,kings kneel blue,
yellows sun compete
a flutter,
a constellation roars
complete!

godmaker

he stood on a diamond,
on existence point;
a sliver of a chip
on the pinnacle of perpetuity
acute with its own dimension,
souled -incandescent!
hued with everything,
he gleamed -

angry death is sulking -
where is the diamond whole?!
of all the gleams that shirk prodigious
in a vast universe without conscience
flooding the master process
delinquent,still profundit'
in competitive altercations,
yearnings absolute -
where is the complete adorn?!
within degree -hypocrisy settling
into its usual rancid wound,
all maggot blessed,
with nauseating swallow-tongued stench accompanied
of old meat and fruits
picked and cut for quick dispose
but gag-reeking for centuries without countermand
this mortal mingle
sucked out soul-tortured provocation
of tribal fidelity still clinging
onto the fatuous misperceptions
of common eternity
when reality rarely solicits immortality
beckoning one final degree of hope
all that glitters was pure
but age still grudgingly relinquishes doubt
that truity and falsity cohabit
a mixed yet bearable marriage
consummated seven thousand blessings;

of all the assorted decapitated holies
vomiting all their virtuous indiscretions
up whores,boys,boundaries and wars
into this bath
washes in a sea of blood
rests these too pitied souls
into the abyss,

deep this eviscerated sea
scrolled and unmeasured
except the weight of one carcass
floating to the putrid surface -
an ass,a lily on the throat
a long wisdom-green-stemmed lily
fully open on the tip
of a point,
a slivered one,
hued with everything,
gleams -

orphan

cat!
inspired!
much battled,raw-eyed glimpse
off the bloodied fashion streets,
a quiet,dry
cut through an unbalanced curiosity -slash!
intractable stray
alley plaintive wail,slashed
lone,lone
strayed
leap!
involuntary
survive!

ravages exegesis perfumed pity-fur
unclings the sad carnage de-tongued
anxious sorrow crouch begs the night
screaming silence into echos
persistent death
creeping lingers
desolate healing wounds,longer
shreds humanity -cut out!
statutory evisceration
clogging arteries,webbed
furtive hordes evolution
disillusioned
cease fired!
revolt!

orgy
tidal-wash bathes this bloody cat
regurged piety dripping weapons
pity-slumber all humanity
smothered shrieks
out from under this rhapsodic harmony splatter
spectrum fulmination vomit-red
covered obliquely volcanic
searching
humanity drips
splash cradle rocks,splash cradle falls
survive!

great stories gathered
small definitions report
threat!

next participation -brief
destiny's uncultured tatoo
infected!
running ink down this zigzag course
civilization's uncanny portrait
mirrored pity this poor,loose-furred cat
shred mimicking history's most unorthodox play
meows upon this stage set most dramas
unnatural course
naturally soft paw
almost painting this play of life dangles
perilously close
oblivion's second nature repeats
the utterance so carefully wounded -
survive!
causation and result
survive!
nature's natural inclinations -paralyzed
consternation has its lock;
jawed and fearless eternity
rascal's its varmint 'pinnings
within its own varied context;
destiny tracks and unponders,
deliberates without causation
unparalleled price and pertinacity

and the cat's meow
mournfully,unmistakenly
reaches out -

wolf

in bloom!
the impatiens bloom
but the wolfbane weeps the night
cant!

sovereign blood-
drip-stark a nation's dignity
salvaged,
metamorphosis,
a talent for kill-
fresh!

evolved!
evolution's mystery -unevolved
incarnate again!
so the dying envy-weep the dead
the eternal corpulent mistress
stark,fangy,naked savage raged
her new calf in jaws
clenched trickling immortality's selective dominion
down the drooly biased chins
of anarchy's self depose
washes civilization's celebrated wretch
all bound by nature
chunk by natural chunk
gory-muggy disposition blues
a groggy moon's desperate cast
the great animal vampire
does gorge soufflé human
lustily chomping
grace through execution of duty
of immortality's playful expectorate
slurping up all the ephemeral excess
lapping up all society's recalling juices
spitting out only the least resistance
verit' -par excellance!
tomorrow's moon,
full again -

peeled!
back the skin of the bark
off the moon's raw,tendered speak
this prickly discordant flex
a tear of sleeping wolf is not
of tender sleeping dreams
eternity's astonishing splintered march

all fulmination bemoans
rapid rivers warping
the great order of continuity
beneath a yellow hooded sheepy hue
following incontinent wretching hope
evolves again
cyclical bargains fanged
randomly snapping trees and branches
post shimmering rampage
bodily heaving
each fallen idol of demagoguery
passing through these trees,this forest
assuming greater posture
grand bristling,rabid posture
set deep in the soul of motion
flesh'ly breeding perpetual motion
tearing satin cool immortality's diamond
to bend its eternal magnificent plume
toward the destiny recant
all this pursues and festers
to lance the moon's only boil
convincingly used the wolf's seduce
these sheep gang lead
to coordinate the maxim fires
of shocking whites and pistil blues
to a dreamy eyed manifestation
in a bed of bloody dripping calf hearts
torn out from soulful lust
under a moon's vengeful curiosity
too noble to noble

ignominious departure
falling far from grace
this crowning crash
to pieces all civilization's mighty mist
of perpetuity's long overwrought dream
consistantly,vaguely discloser persists
the wolf's tracks engage
humanity's inconceivable belligerent spout
denies and contrives
a vision panoramic pertain
of bristled hair and fang
gouged deep in the minds and apathy
of a civilization born brooding sycophantic
still choking of the wretching purity
resolve humanity bequeaths
rest!
let the soul rest its cultured sire
into the hearts compendium,swings

the restless pendulum of many fates
both ways of mercy and merciless
boundaries abound
all subordinate trials —error
significantly lax
the seemingly uncontrollable urge
to born again, to procreate
to recreate the species image shocked against
yet another offering,
another moon,
still aglow
still, unresolved-

zebra

at blink!
the sun's angry shutter
rushes down-shower
a rude awakening all history's past
flood in full-bodied flower,
exposed!
all naked white exhibition
unshadowed
unclothed,
pure unadulterated nude!
adulation appall -

black!
clouds wisdom disperse
soul-blood dripping white images
over smokey crimson aspirations
contorted,diffuse snotty noses
running over cruel misshapen
puffy blistered much centuried lips
shackled souls,puckered density
altruist notions burgeon seldom
desert wanderings,unseen
paradoxical misfortune abound
in snowy revelations fleshy-manifest
eating raw sewage vegetables
all pusy-munch and chewy
history's rotten refuse
feeds back too aged aristocracy
made immortal dead -still dead
the rude awakening clash
of this history's past
awakens -

anarchy!
the gutter's stripes cant
become the mourning glories
all shimmery blue incandescent
bold in that fertile green-sun
unsolidarity sweet kisses
a goddesses sour brooding breasts
pendulous unkind age swings truth out of its unsavory
smack
tainted libations' willful jest at lust
at dawn breaking treachery guilds a nasty corner
old black now beams fresh fruits-glisten
itinerary all map-lived and no direction to go

compass paradox burgeons again solicits
come,come,come
let all the degenerate misshapens'
harmony pose desperate allegations
made pointed through an empty heart
sewing those empty seeds
into a vast tapestry heavily bodied
piled beyond the sky incalculable ineptitude
made virtue elite
but exclusively heavenly rights still held exclusionary
all depths plummeted coexist
seize the dying wind
blast-off the tepid,unwilling
mergers
hold the dying wind;
undead the morning glories,cant
cut the leg-iron misanthropic rust
corroded deep soul,purposed?
but undefined!

launched!
the old ship is off!
slave traders,traders,traders
trade conscience bleeders
down the ship's narrow splintered planks
running,tripping gagging
coughing out history's rewrites
written over the sides of vessels
into the deep sea unspoiled
all rotting larva swim and flourish
putrid,salted,seasoned very tasty maggots
swallow generation's whole
again,again,
the nature cycle repeats;
all seasons vary,change
the dark skies uncast and lift
offshore the waiting fish
all fresh gilled and breathy
retain the order amidst the chaos
and more evolved colors blend and fade
and memory is obscurity
is history forgotten
again remembered differently
at time convenience remembered
comfortable,sullen
still purposed!

dark moon

the air does not breathe
the catch of gold,now dust
does not glimmer;
life fecund —once!
a sea's memory—flamed,
essence too,
up-drifted
ghosts as well —up_sent!
vestige makes
vestige doctrine endures
all but gone
except — except!
one distant memory
linger ——— s!

passion ——- lost!
dispatched!
menacing gods no longer
civilization,
once mercy begged
unguarded;
the ephemeral flesh
now mist
of soul and strained idea'
lost
the urgency of construct
the dawning of effigy
lost
an ocean drifted
so its place,
so its society born,
lost!

once
gods and demons parity
powers scaled,
balanced!
oceans and microbes
from shadows sea-wet
to granules
worn by worn
by wind-drop seditions
exacerbated dreams —uncounciled
into that solitary wink of time
of trickling percipient eyes
of blood and fate and death
comes the daunting circumstance of civilization

wincing and stammering
and stumbling
a stuttering mockery of exist
the briefest thread pause
through this great paradox
fired display constance
as in everything dense
the very paradigm of now
seething and peppering
time's willful energy with equal dissipation
folds into contract
with its own lost,dark seas
with the ill tempered unconscionable disposition
of nature's perfect necessity
fully engendered
fully realized,
fully disappeared!

scant awakenings endeavor
the wry harvest of genius
solitary discourse
plains and solaces
well-up
humanity's most costly achieves
pleading up the angry wind
of darkness and eternal pity
and the clear,well linked passage
to the brighter side
of unbroached futile aspiration;
the body's drip
its constant plea
into this dry ocean
for one last favor
one last arbiter
of social injustice
gone right!
one last clear vision
of trust and unity
and the complete absence
of dominion
and the worthy aspiration
of continuum

tree

soul ground
earth,unaged divide
transect rooted deep
graveyard
sleepy tribal oak
keeping watch
resides
permanently
future

bark!
uncowled century mystique
scarred!
pains civilizations risen
noble peeling
layer from unpitied layer
unsated ancient flesh
sage from absolute
unwise scourge
war!
anti-blood clot -capped!
thirsty still
voracious cycle,again
good/evil
face to ugly face
compromise
destiny's ravaged nerves
bare
raw
open
struck!

cold
icy wind/rain
from a bark's earliest scar
slash whispering wet
idea things
crawling inner ear
curious,urgency
cross cutting century
slowly
seeping to core
ring by disparate ring
cracking civilization's charge of disbelief
into crowns of ploy and anarchy
furtive growth

disperse!
agony's triumphant plow
through these dreams and gardens
bouquets aplumb,a feast
victor expanse!
visions greens and blues unperiled
ever-slow dynamics danger engage
true ideas
take true course
truly occupies these grounds
keepers kept
by a tree,
solemn,unhurried
regard

spikes and apple seeds
wind and fire
scorch a moment
bursts suns and vineyards
dripping cool wines of blood quench swallows
of burn and history
soil deep
into every root
pumping back to core artery
heart/birth/death
rebirth!
center!
civilization's disrupted cradle
rocks and spins
naked antipathy
slouches behind every endeavor
ready to spring on every need
profound and unsympathied
comes to terms
at once
inside the core,
out!

dead prophet

ash!
all seasons flush
larkspur and juniper
fight for light and dew
the piercing eagle devil's its claws
open wing
evocation upon the near-desert floor
once wet,very wet
now dry
. . . . becoming very dry

little shallow waterbed
dying slowly
surrendering its millennia truths
squirming on the silty rocks
unfertile
now broken
light and time enjoin
risen sun -turned
still red,still cold
light strike!
history up!
reach back,
air whip!
crack!
a new season born

laws!
written on stone
asks the right questions
unnests the eaglet in flight
broken shell left in shadows
mists another moist soon to be arid pocket
and so why terminal why
it reveals and then . . . .

human remains
skull and parched soul
left for dead
one extended digit
pointing
to stone,to somewhere
to nowhere
the letters clear/obscure
the words of the letters

from all nations reproach -reprise!
indifference! treason! succumb -
obliquity -obsolete!
flesh and matter shift
all seasons arrival explained
and exits fold brief
into easy scratchings,
comfortable obligatory syntax'is
leaping to first thought
striking the brain's darkest matter
into light
trembly,willful light
desperate colting urge to stride
full gait
on a spitting fury and calm
before the natural setting
designed to awaken
all the sensibilities
dribbling down the toothy mouth
too tired to hunger
too hot to comprehend
too desperate to thirst
too simple to sink into the greater/lesser
of the mind's current fashion
already marked and inviting memory
absence -

the soul ponders the void
derelict compromise,
parting lovers remember
for a short time
the seasons change
and the spindly knees wobble
and quakes and floods occur
from these tremors
all life ripples
its just necessities do not negate
purpose and prophet
summon the gods
risen from these trimmings
take to task
all nature's eventual surmise
and propose!

river

under the goddy tree
all de-fruited and divined,
bears river of blood
flowing branch north,unceremoniously
curving unnatural device
unfettered baby flesh,at foot
coos centuries cry lost!
-the crimson leopard unpaws-

brown wilted branch
arc white
an old man dodders
pearl shock -
flesh wisdom brim'
'quired breathing,soul manifest
momentary exertion
pointing up river
plaintive right
turning apathy appease
child skin/bones
soon scattered ash
not souled
will the dust turn white
to the river
bearing all those goodies
-offering up
will contain
up life!
infant raised and placed
on this bank
child pending,
slash-open!
lightning strike!
fire

doomed prophet!
covered in blood;
offering
baby heart
removed!
at tree root,
buried;
to fertile suffice -
the crackling sound of burnt flesh
break-popping sooty portent
wafting all sacrifice to the greater season

the absolute bond
of flesh and ash and time
in place of all mournful loss
tearful absolute
if ever did exist
traveling soul-darkness pass
through culminating a more plausible front
the dust serves its course
to the whole
to the essence of continuity
to the understanding of discontinuity
healing river,open wounds
profundity splashed
into the eyes of eternal nature
of man,and beast
and ubiquity

cowled in black
undiminished portent
unceremoniously gracious
apotheosis -complete
multiple gifts attributed
distant time
relative time,
relative,absolute time
plays the river music,fertile
without the watchful gaze,
the ever paternal non-entity
the unnecessary pouting ubiquity
of current now in redirect
the dire-unessential spirit
rests
the horrible bloody dawn
casts new distinctive light
alternate course begun
wearing the rocks
embedding the thoughts
coursing law and purpose
through veins all living avail
to the greater life
without divine interrupt
a natural progression
in resolution
in real dimension
in continuity
in transient objectivity
perpetually,obliquely
dispassionately
achieved

scarecrow

silence!
death!

into death petal pollen
scattered everywhere
there is no growth!

covered!
a snow sheltered field
all but level stones and scars
winter's continual sagging paradox
lifts!

grey skies
hint unsheltered
far-sun bursts sea-shell scatter
rebels
not here -yet,
the scarecrow hangs its careful watch -
everywhere!

under blanket
blood on stones
shrill lines obscurred
warred quiet
still lifting
still watched
on vigil
yet!

primary good
secondary evil
incarnate
then withered
intermediary and sundry particles dry
scorched to ash
forgot
vision melted grounds
new!

the uneven molds of destiny
undead,broken here but stayed
ultimate death,
from creased mountain peaks
and utter pity-shallows
from under sympathy-shards ice,return

colder-cold streams between
rocks and bodies and greener-greens
down upon the cities flourish or flood
seasons: spring,summer,
fall,the winter drifts
utter humanity culminates a hue
breathed deeply
observed -

uncapped!
scarcity and harmony
cut!
deep through these false fields troughs
of tears and transcendency
fully explored -

disrupted -
full-hearted burgeoning
exploding tragic myths and rights
beyond terminal forte
by gods diminished made unseated
in their eternal effrontery quest
made simple
too to dust
will remain
covered
and watched,
then?

mute

cold-dark
unseparated humanity
spurring souls unhealed
the shakes
horrific cold-sweat bowl-ings
upright!
post-night clearing!
perilous chest -open!
heaving word silent
thrusting heavily into ghosted dark
uttering speechless volumes
reverberations bouting
through endless haunted souls
transfixed dark
unfixed!
the silent verb
stuttering spirit nature
struck!
voice of gold
the unconscious text
pure thought
delusion undenied
reality unblocked
dimensions horror lifted
light
recalcitrant actions unmute
mad-dog clenched jaws and shards
burn-cut the soul
tender solace,sweet solace,
succulent unladen waiting burgeon cup
most delicious gold
unsavored
sip!
cut!

heavy throated dark
the silent voice
eloquent bloody tragics
speak -
monster nation,looms!
unabated,
unslayed
twisted glory-goul pathings
into iron blood
lacing tormented windfall terror-comfort
weighs burden recur!

a blind bird sings
unspirited callous melody
pierce
dead souls recant
dark musings pervade
under-hell retains
its dead-god recoil
chorus -
pitch in the dark
coda:
uncommon death summons
by angel-wings dint of fate
symphonies spook rebellious dawn
disjointed radicals misbehave
torn
from earth's simplist womb
fury born a different manifest
disease!
rage!
crawling corpse over mangled corpse
in unrepentant contorted dark
cold soul
dead soul
dark

brilliant dawn
pendent dawn
unremitting dawn
sparrow!
the still,unbreathable air
wings -
change occurred
unwatched
stimulated but unmetered
new directions form
unhealed wounds
scar!
dance over old flesh
renewed
spirit flame
rekindled
bursts fire
and dove entangled
interwoven
eternal struggle,
dawn!

things

above seas
above rain
above nature's most purposed intent
the seeds of lightning sew
high brooding naked caliphs
blackbirds wing
wicked soaring exonerate
sweetly tuned percipient pitch
rising,twisting blue blood flutter
highborn indefinite
piercing indeterminate
redeyed cooing doves
ascending throne
clash!
fury risen
dark horror plummet
all things proposed
to the center
to the blackest core
descent
hell,
and then . . .
a chirp
a dainty cry
sunlight teases,
a blink
more -
more chirp,more tears
more light
more magnificent flooding light
all wonder . . . . .
and then?

children of the locust

pirouette -
founder!
off the rising,spiraled,fired plains
darkness opines its bloody portent
in rising
recall!
deep the unforgiving task of mourn
peeping off its different pose
the starving,quivering,unsure dewy-death
kneels and prays in holding
rise!
spirits rise!
still unsrrendered
now war unburdened
ascend!
once escaped
now still -
ascend!

what quiet greatness aspires -
reels!
its turning monster democ'!
the commingling of unbridled tenure
and surreptitious loyal contempt
and deconstruction's lousy end
for the crooked spine of mis-articulation,
what will rise from this soil of this blood,
what tools ordained defense?
falters,slumbered,wicked dark
during sun's unfaltered bright
on this waking dead
from this tomb of unresolve,
advocates come this nourishing predict
of time's lingering languish
of treason's insurmountable
and decimated intrigue;
all set to the soured discourse
to unsour
will predict
another burning star
even stronger now
undimmed by ascent
even more luminous now -
appreciably
ascent!

the timorous,decorous
ill-timed peer -blunders!
of dogma's sterile tenacity -
now in summit declaration
of the lost,ardent pursuit of declaration
of contingents and hypocrisy
embrace for the sad storm of embracement
subside without subsist
to the unburdened pasts
seizing dawn's early pedigree
seizing tenure unrestraint
mingling more tenure unbridled
still burdened -unfettered
for future's galloping distance
the infinite pouring of limited life
into the serrated bowl
of purposeless,purpose
fired ends,immortal simmer
burbling contentions and distance
far,far from star
and destiny
the inane distraught,distillery
brought on,interred
deficit disorder commune with
the once tangy rise of fire
now pervades its own distinguished exist
not failing to spread
to permeate
the most impenetrable senses
deep into the living conscience
settles this infecting life
born different
but still arresting
still living
still in ascent -

the brighter flush of dawn's emblematic discord
still decays,
but promises one more day anthology
of the quiet uncorrupt derision
that so bequeaths
its lonely,disheartened integrity
to the even more desolate
of all spirits settled and wished
the unattended,still in proper mourn
still regarding their property peace
with solemn exclusion
regarding only the most hopeful

to rise and restart
civilization's unconstructed
monikers
once again
structured
once again
begins -